Johnny Appleseed

ISBN 978-0-545-22306-5

Text copyright © 2010 by Jodie Shepherd
Illustrations copyright © 2010 by Masumi Furukawa

All rights reserved. Published by Scholastic Inc.
SCHOLASTIC, CARTWHEEL BOOKS, and associated logos
are trademarks and/or registered trademarks of Scholastic Inc.

12 11 10 9 8 7 6 5 4 3 2 1   10 11 12 13 14/0

Printed in the U.S.A.   40
First printing, July 2010

Johnny Appleseed

Written by Jodie Shepherd
Illustrated by Masumi Furukawa

SCHOLASTIC INC.
New York   Toronto   London   Auckland
Sydney   Mexico City   New Delhi   Hong Kong

This is a story about Johnny Appleseed.
With a name like that, you would think he was make-believe!

But Johnny Appleseed was a real person
who lived more than two hundred years ago.

It was a sunny fall day in Massachusetts, when a boy named Johnny Chapman was born.

The baby had cheeks as red and round as apples.

Johnny's big sister, Elizabeth, was happy to have a little brother.
The children played together with whatever they could find.

And the sun shone,
And the rain fell,
And little Johnny played,
And all was well.

 Johnny's family got bigger. Johnny and his sister were joined by ten younger stepbrothers and stepsisters.

What a busy, noisy house!

Johnny would go outdoors when he needed quiet time. Sometimes he'd walk along the river.

The squishy mud felt good under his feet.

Other times, he would
sit under a tree and read.

Johnny would watch the animals in the wild:

the foxes playing
in the meadows,

the deer dashing
through the woods,

and the birds soaring high
in the wide blue sky.

If he found an injured animal, Johnny would take care of it until the creature was well.

Johnny liked being outside. When he got older, he went to work in the apple orchards, just like his great-great-great-grandfather long before him.

And the sun shone,
And the rain fell,
And Johnny grew up,
And all was well.

Johnny learned everything about growing apples.

He was happy planting seeds . . .

. . . taking care of the trees

. . . and munching on the
delicious fruit.

Lots of people were moving out west back then.
When Johnny was all grown up, he decided to go west, too.

He didn't bring much with him. For a hat, he used his pot, and a burlap sack did fine for a shirt. And shoes? Well, why wear shoes when you have two perfectly good feet!

Johnny traveled the countryside.
The sun kept him warm by day.

The stars made a roof
over his head at night.

The rain washed him clean.

And the animals kept
him company.

Sometimes Johnny would stop and plant apple seeds. As soon as seedlings grew, he'd sell the small plants to families moving west.

When they got to where they were going, the families planted Johnny's seedlings and grew trees of their own!

Johnny was friends with everyone.

Wherever he went, he'd bring seedlings, pitch in with chores, and share stories of his adventures.

The seasons passed. Every fall, Johnny gathered seeds from ripe apples. Every spring, he planted the seeds and passed the seedlings to settlers.

He planted so many apple seeds that before long, people started calling him Johnny Appleseed!

And the sun shone,

And the rain fell,

And trees filled the land,

And all was well.

 Year after year, Johnny tended his orchards,
visited friends and family, and slept under the stars.

Because of him, people always had fresh fruit to eat.
Because of him, the land grew more beautiful.

Johnny Appleseed left behind thousands and thousands of apple trees all across America. Just think—the next apple you eat may be from an orchard that was first planted by Johnny Appleseed!

And the sun shone,
And the rain fell,
And Johnny's story lives on,
And all is well.